EMMANUEL JOSEPH

Silicon Valley vs. Realty Giants, Human Stories Behind Business Strategies

Copyright © 2025 by Emmanuel Joseph

All rights reserved. No part of this publication may be reproduced, stored or transmitted in any form or by any means, electronic, mechanical, photocopying, recording, scanning, or otherwise without written permission from the publisher. It is illegal to copy this book, post it to a website, or distribute it by any other means without permission.

First edition

This book was professionally typeset on Reedsy. Find out more at reedsy.com

Contents

1	Chapter 1: The Clash of Titans	1
2	Chapter 2: Bridging the Digital and Physical Worlds	3
3	Chapter 3: The Human Element in Business Strategies	5
4	Chapter 4: Innovation and Adaptation	7
5	Chapter 5: The Intersection of Technology and Real Estate	9
6	Chapter 5: The Intersection of Technology and Real Estate...	11
7	Chapter 6: Navigating Regulatory Landscapes	13
8	Chapter 7: The Power of Collaboration	15
9	Chapter 8: The Role of Leadership	17
10	Chapter 9: The Impact of Market Forces	19
11	Chapter 10: The Role of Corporate Social Responsibility	22
12	Chapter 11: Navigating Economic Uncertainty	24
13	Chapter 12: The Future of Silicon Valley and Real Estate	26

1

Chapter 1: The Clash of Titans

In the heart of Silicon Valley, tech magnates sit in their sleek, open-plan offices, conceiving innovations that will redefine the world. Meanwhile, on the East Coast, real estate moguls occupy skyscrapers, meticulously planning developments that will reshape city skylines. The worlds of technology and real estate seem disparate, yet their paths frequently intersect, often leading to intense rivalries and unexpected collaborations. This clash of titans sets the stage for a series of human stories that reveal the nuanced dynamics behind business strategies.

Behind the polished presentations and grandiose visions lie the personal ambitions, dreams, and struggles of the individuals driving these industries. The tech entrepreneurs are fueled by a desire to disrupt the status quo, while real estate developers strive to build legacies that will stand the test of time. Both sectors grapple with the complexities of market forces, regulatory challenges, and societal expectations, often finding common ground in their relentless pursuit of success.

One such story is that of an ambitious young tech founder who partners with a seasoned real estate developer to transform an abandoned industrial area into a smart city hub. Their collaboration is fraught with challenges, from navigating bureaucratic red tape to reconciling their differing visions. Yet, their shared determination to create something extraordinary unites them, forging a bond that transcends their professional rivalry.

As their project progresses, the human element becomes increasingly pronounced. The tech founder's idealism is tempered by the pragmatism of the real estate developer, who imparts invaluable lessons on navigating the complexities of urban development. In turn, the developer gains a newfound appreciation for the transformative potential of technology. Their journey highlights the importance of adaptability, resilience, and collaboration in achieving ambitious goals.

Ultimately, the story of these two individuals underscores the broader theme of the book: the interplay between technology and real estate is not merely a matter of business strategy, but a reflection of the human spirit's capacity for innovation, ambition, and collaboration.

2

Chapter 2: Bridging the Digital and Physical Worlds

In an increasingly interconnected world, the lines between the digital and physical realms are becoming blurred. Silicon Valley's tech innovators are pushing the boundaries of what's possible, creating digital solutions that have tangible impacts on our everyday lives. Meanwhile, real estate giants are leveraging these technological advancements to enhance the living and working environments they develop.

The integration of technology into real estate is not without its challenges. There are inherent differences in how tech companies and real estate firms operate, from their organizational cultures to their approaches to problem-solving. Tech firms are agile and driven by a "fail fast, iterate faster" mentality, while real estate companies are often more conservative, focused on long-term stability and risk management.

One compelling story is that of a tech startup that develops an app to revolutionize the property rental market. The app promises to simplify the process for tenants and landlords alike, offering real-time data, virtual tours, and seamless communication tools. To bring their vision to life, the startup partners with a leading real estate firm that has a deep understanding of the market dynamics and regulatory landscape.

The partnership is initially rocky, with both sides struggling to reconcile their different ways of working. The tech team is frustrated by the slow pace of decision-making in the real estate firm, while the real estate professionals are wary of the startup's aggressive timelines and unconventional ideas. However, as they work through these differences, they discover that their diverse perspectives are actually complementary.

Through their collaboration, the startup gains insights into the intricacies of the real estate market, while the real estate firm learns to embrace a more innovative and customer-centric approach. The app's launch is a resounding success, transforming the rental experience for thousands of users. This story illustrates how bridging the digital and physical worlds requires not only technological innovation but also mutual respect and understanding.

The journey of this tech startup and real estate firm highlights the potential for synergy between these two industries. By leveraging each other's strengths and learning from their differences, they are able to create solutions that are greater than the sum of their parts. This chapter emphasizes the importance of collaboration and the transformative power of technology in shaping the future of real estate.

3

Chapter 3: The Human Element in Business Strategies

At the core of every business strategy lies the human element. Whether in Silicon Valley or the realm of real estate, it is the people behind the companies who drive innovation, make critical decisions, and navigate the complexities of the market. Understanding the motivations, aspirations, and challenges of these individuals is key to comprehending the broader dynamics of these industries.

In the fast-paced world of technology, founders and executives are often seen as visionaries and risk-takers. Their success stories inspire legions of aspiring entrepreneurs, but beneath the surface, there are also tales of personal sacrifice, burnout, and resilience. The relentless pursuit of innovation comes at a cost, and the human element often reveals the price of success.

One notable story is that of a tech CEO who, despite achieving remarkable success, grapples with the toll that the constant pressure and high expectations take on their mental health. Their journey is one of self-discovery, as they learn to balance their professional ambitions with their personal well-being. Through their experiences, they become advocates for mental health awareness in the tech industry, fostering a culture of empathy and support within their company.

Similarly, in the world of real estate, developers and investors are driven by their visions of creating lasting legacies. However, the human stories behind these grand projects often involve navigating complex family dynamics, balancing personal values with business interests, and dealing with the inevitable setbacks that come with large-scale developments.

One such story is that of a real estate developer who takes over the family business and faces the challenge of modernizing operations while honoring the legacy of previous generations. Their journey involves tough decisions, moments of doubt, and the constant juggling of professional and personal responsibilities. Through perseverance and a commitment to their values, they manage to strike a balance that ensures the long-term success of the business.

The human element in business strategies is a reminder that behind every corporate decision, there are individuals with their own stories, struggles, and triumphs. By acknowledging and understanding these human narratives, we gain a deeper appreciation for the complexities and nuances of the business world. This chapter highlights the importance of empathy, resilience, and personal growth in shaping successful business strategies.

4

Chapter 4: Innovation and Adaptation

Innovation and adaptation are key drivers of success in both Silicon Valley and the world of real estate. The ability to anticipate changes, embrace new technologies, and adapt to evolving market conditions is crucial for staying ahead of the competition. This chapter explores how companies in these industries navigate the challenges of innovation and adaptation.

In Silicon Valley, the pace of technological advancement is relentless. Companies are constantly pushing the boundaries of what's possible, striving to create products and services that will disrupt the market. The pressure to innovate is immense, and failure is often seen as a stepping stone to eventual success. The culture of experimentation and iteration is ingrained in the DNA of tech companies, driving them to continuously evolve and improve.

One story that exemplifies this spirit of innovation is that of a tech startup that develops a groundbreaking artificial intelligence platform. The journey from concept to market is fraught with challenges, including technical hurdles, funding difficulties, and fierce competition. However, the team's unwavering commitment to their vision and their ability to adapt to changing circumstances ultimately lead to a successful product launch. Their story is a testament to the power of perseverance and the importance of embracing failure as a learning opportunity.

In the realm of real estate, innovation often involves reimagining spaces and finding new ways to meet the needs of modern society. Developers must balance the demands of urbanization, sustainability, and affordability while creating environments that enhance the quality of life for residents. The ability to adapt to changing market conditions and regulatory frameworks is essential for long-term success.

One compelling example is that of a real estate company that embarks on a mission to transform a historic neighborhood into a vibrant, mixed-use community. The project requires innovative design solutions, stakeholder engagement, and a deep understanding of the cultural and social fabric of the area. The company's ability to adapt to community feedback and regulatory requirements ensures the project's success and sets a new standard for urban development.

The stories of innovation and adaptation in Silicon Valley and real estate highlight the dynamic nature of these industries. Companies that thrive are those that embrace change, take calculated risks, and continuously seek out new opportunities. This chapter underscores the importance of staying agile and open to new ideas in an ever-evolving business landscape.

5

Chapter 5: The Intersection of Technology and Real Estate

The convergence of technology and real estate is reshaping the way we live, work, and interact with our environments. This chapter delves into the ways in which technological advancements are transforming the real estate industry and the human stories behind these innovations.

PropTech, or property technology, is revolutionizing the real estate landscape by introducing digital solutions that streamline processes, enhance efficiency, and improve the user experience. From smart homes and IoT devices to virtual reality tours and blockchain transactions, technology is redefining the possibilities of real estate.

One inspiring story is that of a PropTech entrepreneur who develops a platform that leverages big data and machine learning to predict property market trends. The platform provides valuable insights to investors, developers, and homebuyers, helping them make informed decisions. The entrepreneur's journey involves overcoming skepticism from traditional real estate players, securing funding, and navigating the complexities of data privacy. Through determination and innovation, they create a tool that has a profound impact on the industry.

Another story focuses on a real estate company that embraces technology to create sustainable and energy-efficient buildings. By integrating smart systems, renewable energy sources, and advanced materials, they develop properties that minimize environmental impact while maximizing comfort and convenience for residents. The company's commitment to sustainability and innovation sets a new benchmark for the industry and inspires others to follow suit.

The intersection of technology and real
continue

6

Chapter 5: The Intersection of Technology and Real Estate (continued)

The intersection of technology and real estate is reshaping the way we live, work, and interact with our environments. This chapter delves into the ways in which technological advancements are transforming the real estate industry and the human stories behind these innovations.

One inspiring story is that of a PropTech entrepreneur who develops a platform that leverages big data and machine learning to predict property market trends. The platform provides valuable insights to investors, developers, and homebuyers, helping them make informed decisions. The entrepreneur's journey involves overcoming skepticism from traditional real estate players, securing funding, and navigating the complexities of data privacy. Through determination and innovation, they create a tool that has a profound impact on the industry.

Another story focuses on a real estate company that embraces technology to create sustainable and energy-efficient buildings. By integrating smart systems, renewable energy sources, and advanced materials, they develop properties that minimize environmental impact while maximizing comfort and convenience for residents. The company's commitment to sustainability and innovation sets a new benchmark for the industry and inspires others to follow suit.

The intersection of technology and real estate is not without its challenges. As technology evolves rapidly, real estate firms must continuously adapt to stay competitive. This requires a willingness to invest in new technologies, train employees, and embrace a culture of innovation. The human stories behind these transformations often involve overcoming resistance to change, fostering collaboration, and navigating the complexities of implementation.

Ultimately, the convergence of technology and real estate holds immense potential to improve the quality of life for people around the world. By harnessing the power of innovation, companies can create smart, sustainable, and efficient spaces that enhance the way we live and work. This chapter highlights the importance of embracing technology and the human stories that drive this transformative journey.

7

Chapter 6: Navigating Regulatory Landscapes

In both Silicon Valley and the world of real estate, navigating regulatory landscapes is a critical aspect of business strategy. Regulatory frameworks shape the way companies operate, influencing everything from product development to market entry. This chapter explores the human stories behind the efforts to navigate these complex and ever-changing regulatory environments.

In the tech industry, regulatory challenges often revolve around issues of data privacy, security, and intellectual property. Tech companies must navigate a web of regulations that vary by region and industry, requiring a deep understanding of legal frameworks and a proactive approach to compliance. The human stories behind these efforts often involve legal experts, policy advocates, and executives working tirelessly to ensure their companies adhere to regulatory requirements.

One compelling story is that of a tech company that develops a groundbreaking healthcare app. The app promises to revolutionize patient care by providing real-time health data and personalized treatment recommendations. However, the company faces significant regulatory hurdles, including obtaining approvals from health authorities and ensuring compliance with data privacy laws. The journey involves intense collaboration between the company's legal team, healthcare experts, and tech developers. Through perseverance and a commitment to patient safety, the company successfully navigates the regulatory landscape and brings their innovative app to market.

In the real estate industry, regulatory challenges often pertain to zoning laws, building codes, and environmental regulations. Real estate developers must work closely with local authorities, community stakeholders, and legal experts to navigate these complex requirements. The human stories behind these efforts highlight the importance of negotiation, community engagement, and a deep understanding of local contexts.

One notable example is that of a real estate developer who embarks on a mission to transform a derelict industrial site into a vibrant residential community. The project requires navigating a maze of zoning regulations, environmental assessments, and community consultations. The developer's journey involves building relationships with local authorities, addressing community concerns, and finding creative solutions to regulatory challenges. Through persistence and collaboration, the project succeeds in revitalizing the area and creating a positive impact on the community.

Navigating regulatory landscapes is a critical aspect of business strategy in both Silicon Valley and the real estate industry. The human stories behind these efforts underscore the importance of legal expertise, collaboration, and adaptability in achieving regulatory compliance. This chapter highlights the complexities and nuances of navigating regulatory frameworks and the human resilience that drives these efforts.

8

Chapter 7: The Power of Collaboration

Collaboration is a powerful force that drives innovation and success in both the tech and real estate industries. By working together, companies can leverage each other's strengths, overcome challenges, and create solutions that are greater than the sum of their parts. This chapter explores the human stories behind successful collaborations and the lessons learned along the way.

In Silicon Valley, collaboration often takes the form of partnerships between tech companies, startups, and research institutions. These collaborations bring together diverse perspectives, expertise, and resources to tackle complex problems and drive innovation. The human stories behind these partnerships highlight the importance of trust, communication, and a shared vision.

One inspiring story is that of a tech startup that partners with a leading university to develop a cutting-edge artificial intelligence platform. The collaboration leverages the startup's entrepreneurial spirit and the university's research expertise, resulting in groundbreaking advancements in AI technology. The journey involves overcoming challenges such as securing funding, aligning goals, and navigating intellectual property issues. Through mutual respect and a commitment to innovation, the partnership achieves remarkable success and sets a new standard for collaboration in the tech industry.

In the real estate industry, collaboration often involves partnerships between developers, architects, urban planners, and community stakeholders. These collaborations are essential for creating spaces that meet the needs of diverse communities and achieve long-term sustainability. The human stories behind these efforts underscore the importance of inclusivity, empathy, and a commitment to shared goals.

One notable example is that of a real estate developer who collaborates with a community organization to create an affordable housing project. The partnership involves extensive community engagement, participatory design processes, and a focus on addressing the unique needs of the residents. The journey requires navigating complex regulatory requirements, securing funding, and building trust with the community. Through collaboration and a shared commitment to social impact, the project succeeds in creating a positive and lasting impact on the community.

The power of collaboration lies in the ability to bring together diverse perspectives, expertise, and resources to achieve common goals. The human stories behind successful collaborations highlight the importance of trust, communication, and a shared vision. This chapter emphasizes the transformative potential of collaboration in driving innovation and creating positive change in both Silicon Valley and the real estate industry.

9

Chapter 8: The Role of Leadership

Leadership plays a crucial role in shaping the success of companies in both Silicon Valley and the real estate industry. Effective leaders inspire their teams, navigate challenges, and drive innovation. This chapter explores the human stories behind successful leadership and the qualities that define great leaders.

In the tech industry, leaders are often seen as visionary pioneers who push the boundaries of what's possible. Their ability to inspire and motivate their teams is essential for driving innovation and achieving ambitious goals. The human stories behind these leaders reveal the qualities that make them successful, including resilience, adaptability, and a commitment to continuous learning.

One compelling story is that of a tech CEO who takes over a struggling startup and transforms it into a market leader. The CEO's journey involves making tough decisions, fostering a culture of innovation, and building a diverse and inclusive team. Through resilience and a focus on long-term goals, the CEO navigates challenges and inspires their team to achieve remarkable success. The story highlights the importance of visionary leadership and the ability to adapt to changing circumstances.

In the real estate industry, leadership is often about balancing the demands of development with the needs of communities and stakeholders. Effective leaders in real estate are skilled negotiators, communicators, and visionaries who can navigate complex projects and create lasting impact. The human stories behind these leaders underscore the importance of empathy, collaboration, and a commitment to social responsibility.

One notable example is that of a real estate developer who leads a transformative urban regeneration project. The developer's journey involves engaging with diverse stakeholders, addressing community concerns, and creating a vision for a sustainable and inclusive future. Through effective leadership and a commitment to collaboration, the project succeeds in revitalizing the area and creating a positive impact on the community.

The role of leadership is critical in shaping the success of companies in both Silicon Valley and the real estate industry. The human stories behind successful leaders highlight the qualities that define great leadership, including resilience, adaptability, empathy, and a commitment to continuous learning. This chapter emphasizes the importance of effective leadership in driving innovation and creating positive change.

10

Chapter 9: The Impact of Market Forces

Market forces play a significant role in shaping the strategies and outcomes of companies in both Silicon Valley and the real estate industry. Understanding and responding to these forces is essential for success. This chapter explores the human stories behind the efforts to navigate market dynamics and the impact of market forces on business strategies.

In Silicon Valley, market forces such as competition, consumer demand, and technological advancements drive innovation and shape the strategies of tech companies. The human stories behind these efforts reveal the importance of agility, strategic thinking, and a deep understanding of market dynamics.

One compelling story is that of a tech startup that enters a highly competitive market with a disruptive product. The startup's journey involves navigating fierce competition, securing funding, and adapting to changing consumer preferences. Through strategic thinking and a relentless focus on customer needs, the startup succeeds in capturing market share and establishing itself as a leader in the industry. The story highlights the importance of understanding market forces and being able to adapt quickly to changing conditions.

In the real estate industry, market forces such as economic cycles, demographic trends, and regulatory changes influence the strategies of developers and investors. The human stories behind these efforts underscore the importance of market research, risk management, and a long-term perspective.

One notable example is that of a real estate investor who navigates the challenges of a volatile market to create a successful portfolio. The investor's journey involves analyzing market trends, identifying opportunities, and managing risks. Through careful research and strategic decision-making, the investor is able to weather market fluctuations and achieve long-term success. The story underscores the importance of understanding market forces and being able to make informed decisions in a complex and dynamic environment.

The impact of market forces on business strategies is a critical forces such as economic cycles, demographic trends, and regulatory changes influence the strategies of developers and investors. The human stories behind these efforts underscore the importance of market research, risk management, and a long-term perspective.

One notable example is that of a real estate investor who navigates the challenges of a volatile market to create a successful portfolio. The investor's journey involves analyzing market trends, identifying opportunities, and managing risks. Through careful research and strategic decision-making, the investor is able to weather market fluctuations and achieve long-term success. The story underscores the importance of understanding market forces and being able to make informed decisions in a complex and dynamic environment.

The impact of market forces on business strategies is a critical aspect of success in both Silicon Valley and the real estate industry. Companies that thrive are those that can anticipate changes, adapt quickly, and leverage market dynamics to their advantage. The human stories behind these efforts highlight the importance of strategic thinking, agility, and a deep understanding of market trends.

This chapter emphasizes the need for companies to stay informed about market forces and to continuously adapt their strategies to stay competitive. By understanding and responding to market dynamics, companies can achieve long-term success and create lasting value. The human stories behind these efforts provide valuable insights into the complexities and nuances of

CHAPTER 9: THE IMPACT OF MARKET FORCES

navigating market forces in a rapidly changing world.

11

Chapter 10: The Role of Corporate Social Responsibility

Corporate social responsibility (CSR) is an increasingly important aspect of business strategy in both Silicon Valley and the real estate industry. Companies are recognizing the need to balance profit with purpose, and to contribute positively to society and the environment. This chapter explores the human stories behind CSR initiatives and the impact of these efforts.

In the tech industry, CSR often involves addressing issues such as data privacy, environmental sustainability, and social equity. Tech companies are leveraging their resources and expertise to create positive change, from reducing their carbon footprint to promoting diversity and inclusion. The human stories behind these initiatives highlight the importance of ethical leadership and a commitment to making a difference.

One inspiring story is that of a tech company that launches a comprehensive sustainability program aimed at reducing its environmental impact. The program involves transitioning to renewable energy, reducing waste, and promoting sustainable practices among employees. The journey involves overcoming challenges such as securing buy-in from stakeholders, navigating regulatory requirements, and measuring the impact of the initiatives. Through dedication and a commitment to sustainability, the company

CHAPTER 10: THE ROLE OF CORPORATE SOCIAL RESPONSIBILITY

achieves significant progress and sets an example for others to follow.

In the real estate industry, CSR often focuses on creating sustainable and inclusive communities. Developers are incorporating green building practices, affordable housing initiatives, and community engagement efforts into their projects. The human stories behind these efforts underscore the importance of empathy, collaboration, and a long-term perspective.

One notable example is that of a real estate developer who partners with a nonprofit organization to create a mixed-income housing development. The project involves extensive community engagement, participatory design processes, and a focus on addressing the needs of low-income residents. The journey requires navigating complex regulatory requirements, securing funding, and building trust with the community. Through collaboration and a shared commitment to social impact, the project succeeds in creating a positive and lasting impact on the community.

The role of corporate social responsibility in business strategy is a critical aspect of success in both Silicon Valley and the real estate industry. Companies that prioritize CSR are able to create positive change, build trust with stakeholders, and achieve long-term success. The human stories behind these initiatives highlight the importance of ethical leadership, collaboration, and a commitment to making a difference. This chapter emphasizes the transformative potential of CSR in creating a better world for all.

12

Chapter 11: Navigating Economic Uncertainty

Economic uncertainty is a constant challenge for companies in both Silicon Valley and the real estate industry. The ability to navigate economic fluctuations and mitigate risks is essential for long-term success. This chapter explores the human stories behind efforts to navigate economic uncertainty and the strategies that companies employ to stay resilient.

In Silicon Valley, economic uncertainty often arises from factors such as market volatility, technological disruption, and changes in consumer behavior. Tech companies must be able to adapt quickly to changing economic conditions, manage risks, and seize new opportunities. The human stories behind these efforts reveal the importance of agility, strategic thinking, and a deep understanding of market dynamics.

One compelling story is that of a tech startup that faces significant challenges during an economic downturn. The startup's journey involves making tough decisions such as downsizing, pivoting their business model, and securing new funding sources. Through resilience and a commitment to their vision, the startup navigates the economic uncertainty and emerges stronger. The story highlights the importance of being able to adapt quickly and make informed decisions in a complex and dynamic environment.

CHAPTER 11: NAVIGATING ECONOMIC UNCERTAINTY

In the real estate industry, economic uncertainty often arises from factors such as interest rate fluctuations, changes in housing demand, and regulatory changes. Real estate developers and investors must be able to navigate these challenges, manage risks, and seize new opportunities. The human stories behind these efforts underscore the importance of market research, risk management, and a long-term perspective.

One notable example is that of a real estate investor who navigates the challenges of an economic downturn to create a successful portfolio. The investor's journey involves analyzing market trends, identifying opportunities, and managing risks. Through careful research and strategic decision-making, the investor is able to weather economic fluctuations and achieve long-term success. The story underscores the importance of understanding market forces and being able to make informed decisions in a complex and dynamic environment.

Navigating economic uncertainty is a critical aspect of success in both Silicon Valley and the real estate industry. Companies that thrive are those that can anticipate changes, adapt quickly, and leverage market dynamics to their advantage. The human stories behind these efforts highlight the importance of strategic thinking, agility, and a deep understanding of market trends. This chapter emphasizes the need for companies to stay informed about economic uncertainty and to continuously adapt their strategies to stay resilient.

13

Chapter 12: The Future of Silicon Valley and Real Estate

The future of Silicon Valley and the real estate industry is shaped by a confluence of technological advancements, market dynamics, and societal trends. This final chapter explores the human stories behind efforts to shape the future and the potential for innovation and collaboration in creating a better world.

In Silicon Valley, the future is defined by emerging technologies such as artificial intelligence, blockchain, and the Internet of Things. Tech companies are at the forefront of these advancements, driving innovation and shaping the way we live and work. The human stories behind these efforts highlight the importance of visionary thinking, ethical leadership, and a commitment to making a positive impact.

One inspiring story is that of a tech entrepreneur who pioneers a new technology that has the potential to revolutionize an entire industry. The journey involves overcoming technical challenges, securing funding, and navigating regulatory requirements. Through perseverance and a commitment to their vision, the entrepreneur succeeds in bringing their groundbreaking technology to market and creating a positive impact on society. The story highlights the transformative potential of innovation and the importance of ethical considerations in shaping the future.

CHAPTER 12: THE FUTURE OF SILICON VALLEY AND REAL ESTATE

In the real estate industry, the future is defined by trends such as urbanization, sustainability, and the need for affordable housing. Real estate developers and investors are leveraging new technologies and innovative approaches to create sustainable and inclusive communities. The human stories behind these efforts underscore the importance of empathy, collaboration, and a long-term perspective.

One notable example is that of a real estate developer who embarks on a mission to create a smart city that leverages technology to enhance the quality of life for residents. The project involves extensive planning, stakeholder engagement, and the integration of smart systems and sustainable practices. Through collaboration and a commitment to innovation, the developer succeeds in creating a model for future urban development that prioritizes sustainability, inclusivity, and resilience.

The future of Silicon Valley and the real estate industry is filled with opportunities for innovation, collaboration, and positive change. The human stories behind efforts to shape the future highlight the importance of visionary thinking, ethical leadership, and a commitment to creating a better world. This final chapter emphasizes the potential for technology and real estate to work together in creating a future that benefits all of humanity.

book description: "Silicon Valley vs. Realty Giants: Human Stories Behind Business Strategies":

Dive into the riveting world of innovation and ambition with "Silicon Valley vs. Realty Giants: Human Stories Behind Business Strategies." This captivating book explores the dynamic intersection of technology and real estate, revealing the human narratives that drive these powerful industries. From the visionary tech entrepreneurs who redefine our digital landscape to the seasoned real estate developers who shape our urban environments, each chapter offers a unique glimpse into the personal journeys, challenges, and triumphs behind groundbreaking business strategies.

Through twelve engaging chapters, readers will discover how collaboration, leadership, and adaptation fuel the success of these industries. Uncover the inspiring stories of tech pioneers who navigate regulatory landscapes, real estate investors who weather economic uncertainty, and innovators who push the boundaries of what's possible. Witness the transformative potential of corporate social responsibility and the impact of market forces on business strategies.

"Silicon Valley vs. Realty Giants" is more than just a business book—it's a testament to the resilience, creativity, and determination of the individuals who shape our world. Whether you're an aspiring entrepreneur, a seasoned professional, or simply curious about the forces driving today's economy, this book offers valuable insights and inspiration. Join us on a journey through the human stories that power the future of technology and real estate.

www.ingramcontent.com/pod-product-compliance
Lightning Source LLC
LaVergne TN
LVHW020740090526
838202LV00057BA/6150